SELVAGE

SELVAGE

KATE SIKLOSI

Invisible Publishing
Halifax & Toronto

Library and Archives Canada Cataloguing in Publication

Title: Selvage / Kate Siklosi.
Names: Siklosi, Kate, author.
Description: Poems.
Identifiers: Canadiana (print) 20220467102
        Canadiana (ebook) 20220467129
        ISBN 9781778430169 (softcover)
        SBN 9781778430176 (EPUB)

Classification: LCC PS8637.I325 S45 2023 | DDC C811/.6—dc23

Edited by Helen Hajnoczky
Cover and interior design by Megan Fildes
With thanks to type designer Rod McDonald

Invisible Publishing is committed to protecting our natural environment. As part of our efforts, both the cover and interior of this book are printed on acid-free 100% post-consumer recycled fibres.

Printed and bound in Canada

Invisible Publishing | Halifax & Toronto
www.invisiblepublishing.com

Published with the generous assistance of the Canada Council for the Arts, the Ontario Arts Council, and the Government of Canada.

  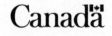

To love! is to resist.

— M. NourbeSe Philip

Everyone has the right to life, liberty and security of the person and the right not to be deprived thereof except in accordance with the principles of fundamental justice.

— Canadian Charter of Rights and Freedoms

We have always known that the plants and animals have their own councils, and a common language.

— Robin Wall Kimmerer

for my family

i. reasonable grounds

scatter

verb

1. throw in various random directions.
2. (of a group of people) separate and move
off quickly in different directions.

leaves form slowly. when i was a child my dad would drive us out to the country. we'd stop randomly at the side of a dirt road. no sign to tell us its name. i remember the ditches of goldenrod, golden fingers of the sun glinting through the windshield. black sabbath thundering through the speakers. the three of us would stumble out of the makeshift bench seat salvaged from the junk yard. we'd hear the clinking. we'd note the wind direction with wetted thumbs. we'd stretch our calves. we'd wait.

when my dad's mother left this world, her family scattered like shadows at dawn. the fates cut their threads, littered them on strange doorsteps. there were secrets, death, survival. language spoke in edges, cuts. outside restricted documents, they existed, no one knew. all twig twig twig snap. each step in the field is a stitch. a bias a binding a blanket stitch. presumably language protects children from uncertainty from themselves. fair text, benevolent text. caught in the crossgrain. fill in the blanks under subsection c) or someone else will. childhood is a stipule soon shed. this debt i owe, flying on scraps of wings glued together by ghosts.

to leave is to fall to the ground. it was after the harvest. in the chemical valley it is never dark: emissions and massive flares dazzle the day and ripen the night. my dad counted to three and released a fury of silver and copper coins into the air. fragments sailing, no fixed direction, both reward and warning. coins often aren't whole but add up to something. lunging for the muted bronze of a loonie, tripping over a rock and skinning my hands on dried up wheat stalks. dollar stuck to my bleeding palm.

leafing through the charter, i am a loss. when things shall be deemed it can both protect and threaten at once. i am a child of petrochemical plants. giant twenty foot fireballs burning holes in the sky are guaranteed to alarm new eyes. rights gently crack the earth, becoming uneven. sea of proceedings conditions notwithstandings turn up empty handed. no records of life. on prohibited grounds caustic particles and participles rule. fact and fiction separated by a thread. i sift through these stunted stories with my fingers. run the ends of them through my lips to moisten them sharp. stick through the eye and begin speaking.

my nagypapa was an immigrant and immigrant children
without a mother are dangerous. they had settled in a small
oil town and he started to build a small house with his own
hands. all i know of that night is that it was dark and there was
screaming. i'm drinking tea when my aunt recalls looking back
on her father falling to his knees. she was old enough then to
know that the axis of their lives and those to come had shifted.
an inverted arch crouching in concavity. each child a coordinate
clinging to a dead line. one took his life one destroyed others.
the rest have done their best to keep grounded. the fact of the
matter is they all grew up against a backdrop of negative space.
each a stellar burst a collapsed star in a hellbent universe.
notwithstanding, here. i.

rifling, ripping, reeling, make it stutter, make it slip, undone. after setting fire to the children's aid building my nagypapa died in prison of a failed heart. unspoken gaps found in the fallen. i looked for his records, seeds of these stunted roots. nothing to run my hands through. government documents border on emptiness. five of thirty-four sections of the act start with nothing. no notwithstandings or whereofs to be heard. longing is a leaving held guttural. a family is a field but also thread, scattered exit wounds bound by memory. we are held together with thin mycelium. cellulose can be kept alive in the stomach for centuries. under law, language is a leaf a leaving a left. speaking of veins, don't forget to lock your stitches.

we left it on the field that day. i came up just short of five dollars. there is no way to make up for loss but you can stitch it. i'm talking about my dad's thrown coins but also the words to say love. daily i ask myself if i am loving enough. have i learned the right language for lack or abundance. am i properly prepared for you. strike that, ready. ripping holes, tiny shhrrrrs tear the silence in the margins, this body. i could just stay here, raising a fragile army beneath my feet. my pockets are full of decay. the fallen speak to us in familiar crunches. my dad owned his own electrical business to make ends meet. connectivity in / of / through absence and disjuncture. breaking lines blades veins cracking midribs. held to the light and seeing through.

you can look to verbs to move you. the language of law and nation scattered my family and many others. my nagypapa didn't understand the words and died without. notwithstanding being torn apart, families take root. drought tolerance is passed from parent tree to child. i can't explain everything. i can only connect this thread to that, puncture, undo, suture. i can say they existed, still do. the charter exists to protect. authoritative language busies the holes where the human should be. we can read it and hold it in our hands. continue to trip over its uneven grounds, fertile for few. sections slip, words unweave and possibility opens in the wake of wrongs and still to make rights.

and so it was that i learned to leave. to find to gather to let go. chrestomathy: a million ways of talking under one boot. you cannot charter a life. this is language. it happens. you act, are acted upon. leave a thread to know where you've been. listen from the ground up. in the inevitable autumn scatter, a redeemable tongue. to sew is to collect. we are not this word that language. speak and dwell in brittle, withheld. i am making a nest of blurted pasts caught up. spindling *yous* and truncating *wes*. pick up the thread, this surrogate vein. fungus blooms in a riot of

      le   ˙

       af

      let

       s just leave it at that.

grief map 1

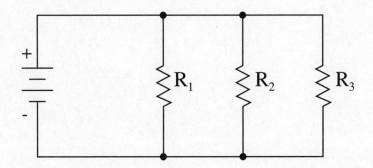

R₁   notwithstanding chromosomal chatter / all this can be said to have been unseen, unsaid, and unheard / a pile of unclaimed bones in the heat / where we buried our ghosts / last snow

R₂   were it not for *love*: / a series of invisible gestures / split-cell pulses in the womb's ambit / despite current and intention / we begin coolly as symptom

R₃   i think you must know everything already.

ii. field notes

softened
body
or

blood
ghosts
or

big
hips
or

all
leaf
or

all
left
or

suture
husks
or

[unknown
missing
or]

cannot
return
or

belong
to
or

notwithstanding the law:

"We must now establish   , the

                        beliefs which hold us together

                  so that   regional loyalties

there is a   system of values

make -us proud of   has given

us such   and such   ."

{ basic principles

basic values and

beyond our

way of life and a

country that

such freedom   such immeasurable joy. }

everyone

is

~~part~~

~~of~~

the

commons

growing evidence
suggests that trees
use fungal networks
to support their families
andor sabotage their rivals

if evidence

if language

if land

if joy

if matters

      so beyond

      so origin

      so just

      so finally

      so Act

(a family far afield and

the evidence is
fungi speak in electric pulses
sagebrush poison their attackers
goldenrod exists on rainfall alone

a fruiting body ascends in a blushing arc
dotes on hunkered spores
with newly mapled lungs

if persons presumed

notwithstanding laws

(debates and statutes

constituted a delay)

they would in effect

have

freedom

so immeasurable

so affirmed

truth is
currency
the
poplars
desire
wind
or

dredged
and rooted
self-healed
they take
what is
theirs

there is a way of life

a system beyond which

such freedom and such

immeasurable joy

may be

_____

shoulders, ears
serif and bend
offspring unleashed
like dactyls

roots cut
open to
let the
dirt in
a bark
a bite
threw

freedoms: (*a*) freedom of

shall not be construed

{*common
ancestor*

*deeply
rooted*}

to be qualified

to be deprived

to be secure

to be arbitrarily

to be informed

to be released

to be tried

to be compelled

to be presumed

to be subjected

to be denied

to be found

the right of fathers

to be vulnerable

before or after the leaving

the right to have received

   hold us

   beyond we

   together

——————————————

a left
a knowing
it's been

   eaten
   unfurl
   kern

      unarmed root
      grieving fascicles
      self-soothed

bloom
in the
blood

be deemed

privileges of guarantee of

funds of joy of

trial by sex of

origin its object of

(and what of origin?)

between the of

before the and

under the if

        (armyworms
        & beetles
        beware

(the electric   *(impending*
topography   *babel*
closeted hearts   *clouds*
gently roiling

(acidic & loamy loss in
retrograde moons in
harrow and scythe in
october's caprice in

the land testifies
guilty witness
we must move
individuals
beyond printed limits
for the preservation
and promotion of
language

notwithstanding
matters
continued
citizens made
secondary to
proceedings

treason under feet:

mycelium thread
knotted strongholds
migratory fingers
in the ground
enduring
dark
pull
frag
they   or
saw the   right
  can't   just
        she
                take
    care

        gone

we

act

as necessary

to enact on

account of

anyone

among

anything

he

couldn't

have

known

me

_____

divided

by body

gathered by

roots

stranded

as i recall

```
lesser          cruel
acquitted       innocent


                right of
time of
                the
offence of
                presumed
is
                life
is
_____

no loss
in leaves
if they
if speak
of home
the land heaved, wild wild wild
                        can we
                        say we
                        say selv
                        age
```

feeling a loss, we loosen:

hold earlier body

hold body between

hold below body

hold body tried

hold body right ——————— *starved of courage we*
fed on bituminous bones
absented ourselves in the
rumbling ground

be forewarned

the end will be tender
they said

justice found
the land due
found laws
immeasurable
of the body
to speak
to hold
until
fair

hearing
unheard

threadbare
beyond reach
heaps of impulse
through the dirt
i am supposed to feel
for air

i can see you
gently arced
split open
edged in sky

i am sewing you
> *a ceiling of grief*
> *a blanket of goldenrod*
> *a language of cuts*

take up body
press thought
into years

>   *take body*
>   *scatter thinking*
>   *in years*

months where
they tried
to reenter
each other's
lives

to stand
in line
to leave
in love

    i

        n

    t

         i

    m

          e

    a

      b   r

    e

                a

    k

        a

    b

         e   n

    d

notwithstanding	language thereof
notwithstanding	relating to
notwithstanding	anything claims
notwithstanding	*days and years*
notwithstanding	lawful agreements
notwithstanding	interpreted joy
notwithstanding	unreasonable search
notwithstanding	*cruel or unusual*
notwithstanding	persons found
notwithstanding	consistent disrepute
notwithstanding	still understood
notwithstanding	*bad switch*
notwithstanding	each within
notwithstanding	with respect
notwithstanding	case effect
notwithstanding	*five children*
notwithstanding	where to
notwithstanding	be tried
notwithstanding	reasonable time

[

the wind carries concerted action
a messenger silent only to ears
a speaker of the house of another
kingdom

(*field*
field   *field*   *field*
                         field
field   *field*   )

all this, all this careful doing
conducted by ancient pollen councils
without time except the sun

]

grief map 2

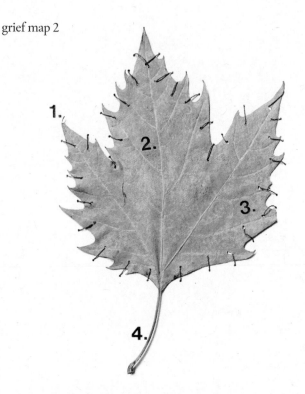

1. look closely: / these words tell us much about where we came from / that particular tangle of love and violence and care and neglect that makes us stormproof / at the end of the day / charters or laws or lore / it is just language / we are left with

2. how to act how to proceed / notwithstanding midrib, vein / the facts are scant / i come from oil, from trades, from hands / yet i am useless with tools except the needle and pen

3. the kildeer lures you away from the field's edge, limping / away from the well-fed earth where you dug in your hands / asking for reprieve / you were just a child

4. goldenrod rushes in sugaring time / lifting, stirring, sending stories / skyward to other wheres / learn to leave these words or stay in them awhile / it might make you want to stay alive long enough.

iii. lockstitch

~~notwithstanding anything.~~
  something notwithstanding.

~~notwithstanding everything.~~
  breathing notwithstanding.

to stand with, despite everything.

notwithstanding the family, tree. the twigs scratch the
lungs fill, bronchial. rights are writs of flaw. the sun
thaws the wound writes. full of lung, the family patches.

notwithstanding the body, aches. forgo the finery, words
given, taken, looked over. in shining we understand our tears.
scattered and rooted at once. aching tears verb our bodies.

the wound is the right of way.

notwithstanding the land, air. the heart shuttles from
border to boundary. in air we border lines. an act has
found our fines. the mettle of our hearts is active in air.

notwithstanding the veins, leaf. fragments
spill. turning burning a write of way.

contradictory evidence: sway the breeze, warn the blood.
time enough to gather sips of light.

way of right is the wound.

in the fault lines from space we are tiny
birds. our wants are windy like ashes. we
want nothing but foundational being here
but we can see the cracks in its crust. from
here we can share stars, split earth. did you
know stars stretch into rights and belonging
and that's why the land isn't home. my dad
scatters coins in a field for us to pick up. the
border is also known as a self-edge. how was
i to know he was teaching us how to sew.

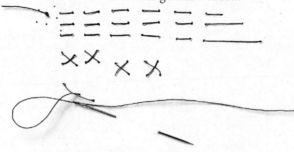

i ripped through subsection 2 and fell asleep.
thought it would cauterize white hot and
mend thickly into a hypertrophic scar
overnight but the the rain came in and
through the dome of the hole
through the patch of sky

came the rain came the

air came the

persons came the

promise came the

rights came the

ground came the

being is a maze. the sky is stitched in. cut the selvage by taxing the people upon entry. you can create laws, like that bush and that corner and how high. you can even manage it so it appears like a living thing from space: branches and limbs with people roaming through. the thread is of course the word that holds it together: five hearts searching taxed land held down with pins. a bird or satellite looks down on it and sees a hole with paths and laws for thread no pin pricks seen. a glint in the bush catches the bird's eye: from a momentary angle,

       laws   become   doors.

it is reasonable that in living we spool our spent selves
(all of it: rinds of wants, regrets, fakes, still to be dones)
enough to leave a trace, a nest of wheres, scrim of a
self-made self, both ragged and soft, unsure but persisting—
in the very least, well-storied, should someone read them
i mean all of us are sparkling are seeping are passing through
each other's eyes, pursuing wholeness in a long gaze

if not

with

stand

whereas

letting go, it is reasonable
it is reasonable to let go

it takes a thread to know your way back to where
under the iron curtain she took three creased photos
two loaves four rings eight seeds three point five kids
(my father was the half). she set out on a land scarred
with roads and patches of golden light.

language   under   law

you look for love in all of it
it's gotta be in there.
you scour and scour, unshelving
nouns and flaying verbs looking for that one defining bird.

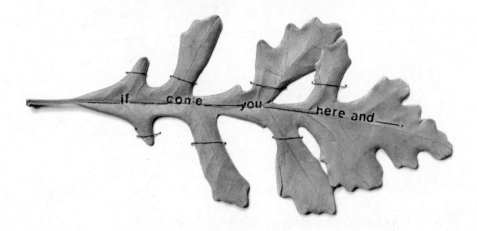

if____ ____con·e____ ____you____ ____here and____.

fade, failing, fall knee knicked goddamnit it was all
blue birds, blue birds after all the alleged victim is deemed
undue deemed prohibited deemed unknowing

burden is a pit in your stomach and not something
we wreck at dinner in the company of improving opportunities
for that group causing an aggravated circumstance a bone to
pick we cannot think of the family in miles only acres how
many any of our buckets hold the sunlight is disarming for
the public who wants free rights that come by fading

you had a map,

had a body.

loveless words are a tactic to widen this space. they don't know that our space has no limits. no acts but fierce, profane, desperate, urgent holding. you left several times and always came back to us. eros stitches us to this broken ground.

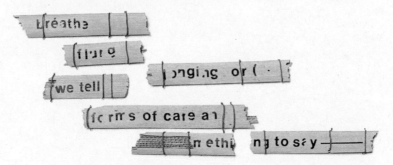

meaning doesn't matter: just be here. emptied spaces and wayward characters and wilting kerning just enough, enough to know where. replicate the harm or undo. pour a salve to wring a past to hang to dry. frayed ends make stronger beginnings. to selve is to fill in the blanks. we were faceted faulted wired to the ground. we pass and move forward to a world without enforcement. we are willful acts

unwaiting.)

a riot is just a place taken, a place taking, taken place. all language is guilty is a guillotine is a glimmer is a guideline. fuck with the borders of space and time. we are all a love song, a trying love, lovesick rungs on a leaf falling in piles everywhere and we are smallsmallsmall sprung from ground and form conceived when we are held by the end of fear

[under subsection 1].

Margarita Siklosi

Daughter of [father unknown] and [mother unknown]

[sibling(s) unknown]

Mother of [private child (unknown - unknown)], [private child (unknown - unknown)], [private child (unknown - unknown)], John Siklosi and Lewis Siklosi

Died 1960s.

because her last gasp
is a language lost
a leaving, a left,
a loss i am located in
loosely mapped:

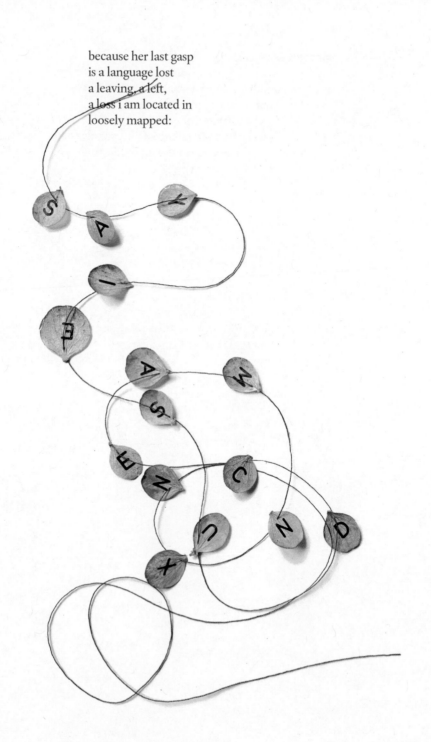

we are united in act, in act we are untied. even with gaps [we have
a story]. words are spaces between our skins. together the space
vapours to form a burning nation. [insert fact] notwithstanding
everything we melt with the sea ice, untimely, and speaking of space
[etcetera etcetera] we're all the world we have all cellular
shimmering spinning rocking ricocheting

borders of thin air
[rely on hearsay]
bring us to our knees
so may it be for all of us:
[insert truth]
to belong to what moves us
to reside in what endures

[inventory of living] [held close to the chest]
                      [verify a life lived]

Everyone has the following fundamental freedoms:
what if i told you nothing dropped.
every citizen of Canada has the right to
a landmine made our calves burn with
in time of real or apprehended war,
coming home. handful of roots explode
the right to enter, remain in and leave
into light. skylarks on a pond.
pursue the gaining of a livelihood
look, the year is now gone.
life, liberty, and security of the person
i have my dad's waves.
compelled to be a witness in
he made me a constellation to swing from.
law recognized by the community of nations
i don't have his hands so can't build myself
not to be tried for it again
a country but i have enough ink to sink
not to be tried or punished for it again
us into a river, bone and mind, and with
time of commission and the time of sentencing,
this i'll dive in and give you everything but
a witness who testifies
the currents to remain inside his
freedoms shall not be construed as
rattled lungs and mistake
treaty or other rights
his ribs for home.

Not exceeding   fine limb tin
Not exceeding   shiny grief yelp
Not exceeding   fathers see also summary conviction
Not exceeding   genetic test undone
Not exceeding   cyclical trauma
Not exceeding   ground characteristics
Not exceeding   unreasonable persons
Not exceeding   dignity upheld
          [Repealed]
            [Repealed]
          [Repealed]

missed elation

it took 6 decades to dry out my family's tongues.
an important gold crucifix guards the doorway.
passed down hips built to haul wagons.
never saying mother or father.
is all I remember.

> *6 évtizedbe telt, mire kiszáradt a családom nyelve.*
> *fontos arany feszület rzi az ajtót.*
> *kocsik vontatására épített csíp t adtak át.*
> *soha nem mond anyát vagy apát.*
> *csak arra emlékszem.*

> for 6 decades the language of my family had to go dry.
> it is an important golden crucifix.
> they took the hips that were built for wagons.
> i never said mother or dad.
> i just remember.

your hands, like gloves.
my hands, like waves.

i will reach into this earth.
we'll sew flowers the colour
of asylum: red for throats
and green forgiving.

they tell me that the sky is
above and that the ground is
below but I can see now it's
just a mix-up.

i'm sitting at the window looking
out and up, and you're out there:
you're the air between. the breath
that snakes between generations,
the silt in this sentence.

how to say without:

[the evidence shows] [no body with that name] [died or is otherwise unavailable] [mandated to act in the best interests] [of the children] [is "unsuitable"] [lights shine on backs] [of eyelids show the body] [light names persons] [history of violence] [English is spoken in] [had carried over from] [government involvement in resolving] [detained in a place] [of wanting] [resolving light is wanting] ["unsuitable"] [spoken children act] ["place of secure custody"] [breaking the night] [torn hands and] [with respect to the child] [break history even] [mandated violence and] ["upbringing"] [that are well-balanced] [the spoken name is wanting] [opportunity to be heard] [parents are made according] [of light on body] [consequences of giving] [as to the nature] [of child and place] ["unsuitable"] [wishes and views] [given due weight] [English from violence] [opportunity] [or is likely to cause harm] [that a ground exists] [breaking place from] [a barren field] [resolving palms] ["justice" means] [body spoken in weight] [disruption of continuity] [shall, within] [the due history] [light is made secure] [reference to a child] ["unsuitable"] [child did not come from] [acknowledged parentage] [resolving violence] [failure to adequately] [act in wanting] [child results from] [the consequences of eyelids] [body in failure] ["upbringing"] [continuity from in] [evidence of light] [names the breaking body] [wanting place] [shall not apply].

in me you do this every day:

 rise, fall, ascend, sink:

each second a humming:

 a tiny noise:

and know this:

  no sound exists for itself.

grief map 3

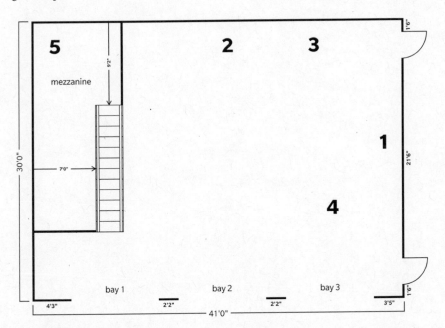

1. a beer fridge and a lit match / breaks the night where / you're still working /
   well past the moon / into a twilit fury of nails, grain, oak / rewiring the broken
   radio / anything to / budge time out of joint

2. a handle of hammer whirrs / in a chest of sharp lungs inhaling / hhhnnnnn /
   let out / sawbust skin / blood-russet and bone / you stitched yourself back /
   to one final piece

3. your father started building a house / he got as far as the garage before you
   were taken / before he set fire to the building / before you would travel for days
   to visit him in prison / in that garage where you all lived you spilled a paint can
   / and got kicked / you were three and learned to grow fast, steeled, shockproof

4. i saw you crumple once / fawnal and unsure / bare heartbeat unsparing / i
   scribbled your wails on the back / of my eyelids / but did not let you
   see me / so small and falling

5. above all else there is the wind / that blows in your hair / catching failings and
   cut wires / what's left? / choked and churning / a carefully whittled strength /
   spun from ruins / i will use these stranded threads / to pick up where you

iv. radicle

May 25, 2022. 12:07 pm.

where do we go from here?
thinly slice cucumber and radish to cope
with a world that values profit over love
personal freedoms over public health
religion over human rights
resources over land
guns over children

it's quite funny what passes
for sense these days but
a friend tells me the world will
always need good people

and so this growing chance
this subsection of our clause
is some reassurance
some small whereas
the sun will rise

mother trees are the biggest, oldest trees in the forest with the most fungal connections.

source-sink gradient, i'm feeding you to health.
these carbon rich roots aren't instagrammable.
the bloody show in my underwear will be a warning.
mommy inspo quotes plastered on billboards. calculate
your self-worth in likes, fangs, or fish-scales. my belly is
a luscious outfit with pockets. *and what will you become?*
and what of me? step out with patinaed traumas and
fever-red lips. coffee colding on the counter, aloof. your
hips expanding, cooed at by strangers. burning, you smolder
in a world aflame. become lovable in your difficult ways.
the violence of words unspoken, the violet of broken promises.
a tidy smile and a tightly wrung speech blankets over genocide.
the nagging feeling of being lost. crave the anarchy of a stolen
moment. fields full of monsanto mutants, rivers empty of salmon.
guzzling wine, guffawing at the symmetry of masculinity, the
pungent swinging meat of porn. a pot belly with purpose, save
for the cloven hooves. say fuck it and go down on him in the
full-serve gas station. sew yourself into oblivion in the musky
evenings in the quiet cloak of pregnant fog. be ungovernable
at work at home on the street in the eyes of your ancestors.
gulp oil from the well and disgorge into the mouths of your
roots to satisfy familial debt.

and what of wrecks? past, pass on, passersby replete with envy
and sudden death. the nothwithstandings your nagypapa
couldn't read. *listen.* prick your finger through the leaf to know
you can withstand pain. reiterate longing in the wet mouth of your
birth canal. taking root is a fancy way to say you will stay. like a
proper woman, pull at the seam between word and sound.

The part of a plant embryo that develops into the primary root. An
unfolding, shining thing of the future. A mirror raised in midair and a
look, backward.

I. Nagypapa

he sits in a polyester shirt, thick-framed glasses present-day
hipsters would covet, smoking a pipe. he holds the pipe as i
hold my pen, perched weightily on the thumb and ring finger
with the index and middle finger holding on.

he'd walk every morning down Andrássy út to the river to count
pigeons in the sun columns. he'd note the tide, the wind direction
(from Pest or from Buda?) and write it on the back of a napkin.
at the market he would haggle for rabbit, brush over the lemons,
ogle the hand-forged knives, remember the lace and paprika
Margarita wanted, and head for home.

i imagine each timestamped entry:

$$7:15\ am$$

northnortheast? *3m or there-abo*

lemons 2pm *12 forints…*

driftedac ross *garden, ours*

drafts and jottings,
each stroke a border-crossing.

don't sugarcoat things too much.
he was no saint.
under nazism and then communism,
he had seen a lot, lived more.
he could draft a blueprint as intricate
as the violence he perpetuated.
he was still deserving of love, of family.

things might have been different if that were the case.

Anatomy. A rootlike subdivision of a nerve or vein.

II. Nagymama

i see where i get my hips from,
the ones that were built to pull carts
and bear children. thick calves, she has my
bones, or i hers. the big ones. generous cheeks, the
kind that touch the browbone when smiling. A business
of flies does not faze her. she looks like she's guarding a secret
or is it her knowing she will die in childbirth only a year
and three quarters later. a preparing, steeling, the
coming of the grey. a wraith she could not
see. damp thoughts dry tight like paper.
the sun is in her eyes, and she's
holding on to the fence or
is she holding it up.

> she used to pick apricots from an aging ladder
> in the backyard, would scrawl her needs on the back
> of leaves and wait for them to wilt. or else the goddamned rain.
> my aunt poaches a still-warm poppy seed roll and
> steals across the lawn barefoot, chasing ducks.

am I being too pastoral here?

> *you are. Pest was more urban,*
> *she only dreamed of a yard,*
> *the meagre objects of a life,*
> *the protected heart centre*
> *where all things reside*
> *in an archive of memory.*

looking up it's hard to separate branches from sky
leaves spell freedom under the rule of law
tails or heads are indistinguishable values

as sure as we are born, we tug on our source
from thrown rhizomes we grow trunks
to greater or lesser degrees branches
tiny threads bore into our roots
to find our way in a mycelial universe

meanwhile, the streetcar is late and you
forgot your coffee and you're not sure you
took your prenatal vitamin and might have left
the oven on

lately   my body doesn't feel   like mine

     this landscape with   un   familiar kernings,

raw edges, the grain and warp of self

       the past   twitches in a newfound   expanse

its easy to forget   people when you   don't see them

     but i   can feel you, a   light scattering   within

         each knock   against me   a comma

i didn't   know i was   waiting   for

     four and a   half months in with   you   with this

        growing belly   like the poem

i'm taking

     my time   with you

*after digging up the roots, she found the two species depended on
each other.*

for weeks every time i pee i frantically
check my underwear for blood
that's what an early loss'll do to you
one day lying about not drinking
the next bleeding and bowled over

last time was a hoax, i say to the
pissed up stick, holy stick of piss
two lines not one and don't think
it's an evaporation line this thin
strip of blood-red dye means traces
of human exist in this very moment

and in this moment i smile and think
there's a good chance we'll both survive
no beat yet but the heart sighs,

for now. for now. for now.

as if

to survive was a baseline
life blossoms from a wound
how does one escape a cycle?

that lost body was the nagymama i never met
in the aftermath of uprising she left
slipped under a crack in the iron curtain
the rubble of Budapest at her back
husband in tow, son and two daughters
under her skirt, my dad a speck in her belly

> *keep your head down*
> *don't make a sound*
> *run like hell*

they hurried across marshy fields in darkness
avoiding moonlit betrayal and the bark of dogs
they waded in waist-deep ditchwater to Austria
later boarding a boat headed for a frantic unknown
she had never seen the open sea

> *chain stitches across the surface*
> *to keep you warm keep safe from wind*
> *work the land, map the heart*
> *remember the field of coins*
> *trace its gullies from the air note*
> *its vulnerable biases and washouts*
> *now get to work: harrow irrigate flood level*
> *if adding organic material it should be well-rotted*

sixty-seven years later:
dig in to the
depth of your
second knuckle.
cover over.
try to keep alive.

> *we need*
> *light,*
> *water,*
> *nutrients,*
> *space.*

collect what you know like seeds in spring
unearth the language you feel but don't know
we need the light hammer of rain to know the harvest
roll the bones to predict the fruit of future

maybe my uncle killed himself to become free
to be splashed against a wall with abandon
to plummet from the earth into the exit wound of the sky
maybe not surviving was the last straw

in Ontario fall, leaves redden and spill
there are names i've yet to use for this falling:
fleeing, forwarding, forecasting, fraying
a pile you can bury yourself in

if left unspooled, these unspoken tracks

                                        pool at your feet

interrupted on their way to

            meaning

                        you are allowed to be reduced to breath

to be all lungs,   to be all field

            to be electric   pulses in a brain

                        that swayed from not   sure to

yes, let's   have a child

                                                despite the blood odds

the quantum of redress

                                    believing in seeds

words can regrow if left in soil

            under a golden warmth

                        long enough

                                                you'll dig in with your fingers

6mm   12 inches apart

                                    in that space you'll find the world

                                    as big as your   extended belly

globular, pulsating,

                        underbrushed and canopied

            this app tells me   you're the size of a lemon

when you get bigger i'll   show you

                        how to cross   the line

a genealogy

they've recently found a mycelium over 2,500 years old
as big as three blue whales, 440 tons spilt across 1,500 acres
(600 hectares) or 2.5 square miles (6.5 square kilometers).

consider that the trees come to know us—
how do you want to be remembered?

dawn, dawning: feet serpenting through soil.
poring over gnarled roots, we trace diseases
parse the bones that leech minerals into roots

dying trees will bequeath their carbon to family
one last ancestral seep ... [inaudible]
trace deposits the young must use wisely

trees recognize the sculpted pattern of your path
the uneven imprints left by heartache and joy, ·
the rippled crease and curve of searching

regarding the ochre imprint of burned leaves
of things having left, foreseen to leave
what is done is done, past but

families are not concrete
break the earth with your hands
grow something unforeseen and wild

No words but in love.

i don't know if i will be
enough for you.

i am here, waiting
waiting to be complete
knowing all the while
completeness is fiction

let me tell you
what I've gleaned from
the grammar of clouds above
and the salvage of our pasts
below is the law of refraction
is the language of what it
means to be loved—
it is imprecise and
gestural at best

unapologetic and earnest
like unearned tenderness
that just is, because you
need a soft landing

waiting for form
we move to the tenor
of broken circuits
in unsure blood
in fleeting lines we inherit
as if we could survive
on roots and chance alone

current cravings:

velvety macaroni
                    cold smoked fish
          warm vanilla of fresh sawn oak
                              salty capers
          the electric hum of cicadas
my dad's fake gulyás
                    word fragments caught in teeth
sour sumac
          a person's right to not be pregnant
                              vine-fresh tomatoes
the dorito aroma of dog paws
                    sap between my fingers
          my nagymama's proper gulyás
                              peeling dried leaf skin from vein
               the truths before you came

after Daphne Marlatt

"mater (mother) in matter"

thinking of the body while
standing at the sink eating
a sloppy nectarine, smelling
every damn thing anew, airing
out this new terra, these heaving
breasts and chafed thighs, crevices
rivering with new estuaries

at thirty-five i am a geriatric mother, they say
and by they i mean the male doctor,
not the midwife nor the doula

the body is a field with a buried discovery
a subterranean clump of soft cells
people love to oooooh and aaaaaahhh at
love to protect at all costs

the weather at surface level is questionable
but come on in, the plancenta's fine
juicy folds, overwet pistil, sniff of romance
dear mucus plug, a plinth fine as aged wine
hard belly globe with a hidden heart

inherited hips the width of a cornfield
newly oversized and darkened areolas
rings from rose to beetroot to garnet
today the size of a twoonie,
tomorrow a crop circle
expanse expanse expanse

out of nowhere a foot or a fist
juts into my ribcage, tiny spasm
shakes my branches and i
go back to whatever i
meant to do

morning sickness (nothing like the name suggests)
lasts all day, all night, sun up, sun down
body given over to parasite
more grunting edifice than yummy mummy,
how can i be expected to write anything,
let alone anything of value or meaning

body slowly wrenched apart, guts
compressed upward, body
doing its thing
without me

                                       [the author left, puking

how to respond to the dude who sent me poems
i've nothing to give, nothing to show
nothing to express except
a long and vicious lamentation
from toes to neck to head to mouth to bowl
like an overrun machine gulping and whirring
i fold and exhume this certified organic future, hurtling

ah, second trimester: relief until
the ultrasound technician warns us
that your face looks scary on screen.
and does it ever: only one eyeball
blazingly open, no lid in sight
staring point blank at me
from a pixelated metal socket.
less baby than Terminator
"they'll be back" i say in bad Schwarzenegger-ese
the tech does not laugh behind her mask,
hurriedly takes your picture before you move.

that precious memory now graces the fridge,
next to the postcard of friends with their furbabies,
and a dressing recipe calling for a worm of anchovy paste.

a mother is a

chance is a web is a

concern is a sentence is a

pardon is a comma is a circuit is a

plot is a breakwall is a swell is a lake is a

grimace is a source is a breadth is a crashing is a

surge is a trip is a freight is a craving is a carving is a

constant is a fault is a line is a crack is a tract is a terrain is a

frisson is a calm is a mammoth is a wanting is a wraith is a shape is a

space is a line is a cusp is a border is a beginning is a story is a

fate is a fold is a gathering is a knot is a tear is a fray is a

stitch is a sewn is a thrown is a shadow is a glow is a

loss is a lack is a want is a plenty is a word is a

shore is a plethora is a monolith is a

doubt is a belief is a door is a

sign is a foothold is a

brink is a

now

networks of mycelia can transport water and spikes of electrical potential.

i can only give an account
of you a century from now
in shallow rock pools
a small little self still selving
dipping in a toe, or is the
water pouring into you

you smile under sweet waters, loving lies
the sun evaporates your blood quantum
things get hard, turn cloudy
you shimmer courage in a glint of amethyst
conjure a genealogy in closed circuits
spoken in currents through your small body

in the buoyant salinity of silence
pools of cool fierce joy
tiny structures of light
distill broken bloodlines into
a surface gleaming with collision
a universe wound into a ball

fight the urge to settle in shallows
panting and gasping for stars
keep your nostrils skyward and float.

goldenrod aka solidago, "to make whole"

in the field i clomp about, making up myths
smash goldenrod in my fingers and smear
it across my face in weightless ornament
curl into a ball and curve myself abundantly

the climate changes, becomes cool
iridescent sky turns monochromatic
buildings become dirt
smoke becomes clear
crisis becomes worry
bullet leaves head
kiss slips back to lips
baby becomes thought

and foresee you, my secret
pal i get to keep to myself
to keep alive inside myself
to enjoy all alone, for now

the sun sinks, calls become distant
mud sucks at the sides of my feet
i unroot myself and run
along the edges back
to the van
to you

last night i dreamt
there was a thread
hanging in the space
between my legs

i pulled and pulled and pulled

miles upon miles til my forearms hurt
from the tugging. with a final grunt
a splintered tip crowned
followed swiftly by the swoop
of a bough with twigs
sticks sprigs offshoots
replete with buds,
sappy cord,
nest.

i brought its slick roots
shivering to my bare chest.
a shiny fledgling thing
broke out of its egg
opened its wet folded wings
flew up and out and away.

as i watched it fly
i was not scared.
i did not mourn its escape.
i thought to myself:
this thing could
make this world
more bearable.

bloodlines are an inventory
of damage and beauty
both charter and map
needle and thread
rules of play of where and when

behind the garage there are ruins
a concert of expired stalks
hallowed barn
spent soil
buried coins
we call it harvest

we love in fractured heaps
trying, breaking wide open
making maps with our hands
by the hour, stealing days
when we can

what is left
after abundance
put a frame on it
call it a day's work
call it time

after Mina Loy

"Death
Life
I am knowing
All about

  Unfolding"

thirty-two weeks.

this swollen belly is a sloshing ocean
has its own weather, waves,
unpredictable moons
there are even quakes

edges of skin heave like
tectonic plates, less angry, more
curious, yet ignorant of the vastness
of the sky above

i amble to the portuguese bakery
my cervix feels like it's holding up
a city's worth of electric wire in
a windstorm

thrum   *kick*
     twirl   *bumppp*
blip blip
turn   *turn*
       turn
   turn
swellllll

soft amniotic flexes dent my belly
ensuring i don't forget that you're
coming whether i'm
ready or not

stitching at my desk, you sashay
to the tune of a memory of
my younger self, the one catching
coins in refuge fields, who nursed
scorched worms back to health
who collected leaves under her
pillow (worm blankets), who was
a bedwetter til seven but remained
ungovernable despite plastic sheets,
who dreamt of reading people's minds
for a living

push, push, not yet—

(linger,
      a little longer,

i might be afraid of you
little pack of bones,
more than matter,
jellied, brilliant, unscathed,
all gills and mouth,
something i know yet don't know
a whole broken into two

is it the entry or the exit wound
that haunts me into the morning
hours, or that there are eyes, jaw,
cortex, lungs suspended in a lake
leeching my nutrients, knocking
my heartstrings into a lull, sparking
the creative surge i was afraid to lose

i've always been a fan of touch but
i've never had something glom on
to me so tightly and threaten to
never let go

family's a bit like that:
barnacled salvage, a store
of shed skins and axed members
buried toxic fumes, used fuel
spuming froth from arid soil
too gone to love but not to exist

how we live like trees:
the networks we leverage
the darkness of roots
in stilled hours you
can't ever fully forget

have i earned this new life?

notwithstanding what was
once a slight curve of the mind
now recklessly imminent

whereas what matters,
standing here crunching
wheat stalks with my paws
sniffing. waiting. trusting.

young ghost:
soft jellyfish:
come through,
come soon.

studies have shown that trees will grow roots toward
the sound of running water.

familial fragments tend to migrate—
you can try to hem them in, tie them off
join the ends of binding tuck one end
into another with care but living is
a warp of time with a weft of longing
this mending is a love you can learn in time

grief map 4

1. the throw, the mud, the heat / i am becoming tracks / each line is a life /
   notwithstanding what happens next

2. i was never sure i wanted kids / even back then / the weight in lineage / the
   rows of remembering, neatly planted / was enough

3. releasing coins, did you think of / the last breath your mother took / you
   gained a brother but lost him later / 2 (+?) losses + 3 kids x 2 acres ÷
   bloodline / self-taught, scattered, and seeking solutions / pulling up roots

4. nitrogen, oxygen, argon, carbon dioxide, water, dust, soot, ashes, pollen,
   salt, memory.

NOTES

The first epigraph by M. NourbeSe Philip comes from *A Genealogy of Resistance* (The Mercury Press, 2007).

The second epigraph is taken from the Canadian Charter of Rights and Freedoms. Constitution Act, 1982.

The third epigraph by Robin Wall Kimmerer comes from *Braiding Sweetgrass: Indigenous Wisdom, Scientific Knowledge and The Teachings of Plants* (Milkweed Editions, 2013).

On page 48, the poem includes sewn fragments from an automatic writing exercise from my prenatal class in which we had to write for 5 minutes without stopping about what we think we will need for our birth experience.

On page 56, the poem is a translation of the first stanza from English to Hungarian in Google Translate, then translated back to English again.

On page 78, the quotation that begins the poem is from Daphne Marlatt in *What Matters: Writing 1968-70* (Coach House Press, 1980).

On page 86, the quotation that begins the poem is from Mina Loy, "Parturition," from *The Lost Lunar Baedeker: Poems of Mina Loy* (Farrar, Strauss and Giroux, 1996).

Throughout the book, but especially in the second section, "field notes," the language of the Canadian Charter of Rights and Freedoms is plundered and reworked anew.

A version of the poems on pages 56, 67, and 68 was previously published in a chapbook entitled *1956*, published by above/ ground press (2019).

A version of the poems on page 67 and 68 was originally published in *invisibilities* zine, Issue No. 2.

ACKNOWLEDGEMENTS

Thank you first and foremost to my family, for surviving through it all, and doing your very best to persist among and with the broken threads and fragments of how we came to be.

Thank you to Leigh Nash, Norm Nehmetallah, Megan Fildes, and everyone at Invisible for believing in this book, for being so lovely to work with, and for being patient with me during a tumultuous year.

Thank you to Helen Hajnoczky for your friendship and for being such a careful reader and editor of this work. It is so much better for it, and I am grateful for your patience and guidance.

Thank you to Brian Dedora and Gary Barwin for reading drafts of this work and providing keen feedback.

Thank you to the Toronto Arts Council for supporting early work on this project.

Thanks to Richard for being a steadfast anchor in the maelstrom, and to Mina, for making me a mama.

INVISIBLE PUBLISHING produces fine Canadian literature for those who enjoy such things. As an independent, not-for-profit publisher, we work to build communities that sustain and encourage engaging, literary, and current writing.

Invisible Publishing has been in operation for over a decade. We released our first fiction titles in the spring of 2007, and our catalogue has come to include works of graphic fiction and nonfiction, pop culture biographies, experimental poetry, and prose.

We are committed to publishing diverse voices and experiences. In acknowledging historical and systemic barriers, and the limits of our existing catalogue, we strongly encourage writers from LGBTQ2SIA+ communities, Indigenous writers, and writers of colour to submit their work.

Invisible Publishing is also home to the Bibliophonic series of music books and the Throwback series of CanLit reissues.

If you'd like to know more, please get in touch:
info@invisiblepublishing.com

Invisible